# 101 Herbal Remedies for Cough and Cold

AF529928

**Dr. S. FAROOQ**
M.Sc., Ph.D. (Gold Medalist), D.Sc., F.R.S.H. (London)

CBS

**CBS PUBLISHERS & DISTRIBUTORS**
4596 / 1-A, 11 Darya Ganj, New Delhi - 110 002 (India)
E-mail : cbspubs@del3.vsnl.net.in • Web : www.cbspd.com

ISBN : 81-239-0829-6

First Edition : 2002

Copyright © by Author

All rights reserved. No part of this book may be reproduced or transmitted in any form or by any means, electronic or mechanical, including photocopying, recording, or any information storage and retrieval system without permission, in writing, from the publisher.

*Published by :*
Satish Kumar Jain for CBS Publishers & Distributors,
4596/1-A, 11 Darya Ganj, New Delhi - 110 002 (India)

*Production Director :* Vinod Jain

*Printed at :*
Asia Printograph, Shahdara, Delhi - 110 032

# Preface

Common cold is the most commonly occurring minor ailment affecting human beings all across the globe irrespective of social strata, geographical barriers hence the name is common cold. It is named cold because mostly it occurs at the arrival of cold weather or on sudden exposure to cold atmospheric condition. Medical name for common cold is Acute Coryza. Because cough invariably follows common cold. Therefore, in common parlance the name cough and cold is used. Cough and cold can be cured as well as prevented from occurring if necessary precautions are taken and there is some understanding of its symptoms and causative factors. Hence this book will essentially serve the purpose by giving brief description on the following.

1. To recognize the symptoms of cold and cough.

2. To find out what are the causative factors.
3. Prevention and non-medicinal care etc.
4. 101 formulations for making home remedies to cure the disease.

I being a Govt. recognized technical-hand, formulating and manufacturing Ayurvedic herbal compounds since last 22 years, have formulated some herbal compounds successfully which were well accepted in the world market. I delivered talks and presented papers in national and international conferences about the efficacy of the simple drugs having holistic approach. Being fascinated with this I thought that I should jot down my experience to help people at large by presenting these simple remedies in the form of this book.

By using these simple herbal remedies one would not only save money but also get cured without facing many side effects of modern medicines containing harmful chemicals, preservatives and artificial colours. Scientifically these formulations are proven, safe and efficacious and time tested as per Ayurvedic textbooks. These are successfully used by Pharmaceutical companies, ISM/Medical practitioners and folklore. If they can, why not you.

# Contents

# 1
# What is Common Cold and Cough

Breathing involves inhalation and exhalation of air. Infection denotes undesirable entry of pathogenic microorganisms into the body. We normally inhale healthy air if the atmosphere is clean; and we are not surrounded by infected or ill people. If we are in dirty atmospheric conditions like near drains, garbage and filth or are in contact directly or indirectly with a sick person, we can contract disease by inhaling pathogenic microorganisms that causes respiratory infections. Throughout the day and night air laden with dust and germs is passing over the mucous membrane which lines this system of tubes and really it is not surprising to find that it is one of the commonest sites of infection.

Common cold is a catarrhal disorder of the upper respiratory tract which may be viral or an allergic reaction, and marked by acute coryza, slight rise in body temperature, chilly sensations, general indisposition and bodyache. It usually gets complicated due to super added secondary bacterial infection.

A cold is an infection by a virus of the respiratory tract which extends from the nose and mouth via the larynx or voice box, the wind pipe or trachea, the bronchi of the lungs, branches of the trachea, and smaller divisions of the bronchi to the lung tissue itself. It is usually accompanied by sneezing, coughing and shivering.

Cold is sometimes also called as Chill. Chills and colds are the commonest illnesses in the world. Exposure to a draught of cold air, sudden immersion in water, or wetting of the feet on a cold day may be predisposing factors. This condition usually caused by a virus, therefore antibiotics have no effect on simple cold. It is only when there is super-added bacterial infection then the antibiotics may be required. A cold in the head is associated with nasal catarrh. The catarrh sometimes extends into the frontal sinuses causing headache or in children, it may spread up the Eustachian tubes causing inflammation on the middle ear and painful earache. When the throat is affected, the tonsils may become inflamed. If the virus spreads to the lower end of the respiratory passages, bronchitis follows. Coughing indicates that the air passages in the region of the larynx are having irritation and/or contain mucus. Coughing is a series of expulsive expirations which attempt to force the irritating mucus up into the mouth, from where it can be expelled out. For common cold bed rest is often beneficial.

## TYPES OF COUGH

The word cough denotes expulsion of air with a sudden opening of the glottis and a characteristic sound. Coughing is a symptom of respiratory disease.

We have different kinds of cough e.g.

1. Cough associated with Bronchitis
2. Whooping cough
3. Coughs and Heart disease
4. Stomach cough
5. Nervous cough
6. Smoker's cough
7. Croup
8. Cough associated with Bronchial Asthma

1. **Smokers Cough :** The cigarette smoker often develops a hawking catarrhal cough due to irri-

tation of the mucous membrane of the throat and clears up entirely when smoking has been discontinued.

2. **Nervous Cough :-** Any cough for which no reason is found is called nervous cough. There is no disease for these coughs. Some people always cough when they have to speak or read in public.

3. **Stomach Cough :-** It is due to irritation of the food passage or the back of the throat. The conditions which cause stomach cough are indigestion, diarrhoea, constipation, worms, decayed teeth, trouble with wax in the ear, enlarged tonsils and adenoids.

4. **Croup** is a condition of the infants and children, due to inflamation and obstruction of the larynx by allergy, foreign body, infection, or new growth, marked by a resonant persistent barking cough.

5. **Coughs and Heart Disease :-** Certain diseases of the heart are accompanied by coughs; eg; inflammation of the membrane covering the heart-pericarditis; is sometimes accompanied by a hard, painful cough. Aneurysm of the aorta is usually associated with a typical bassy cough

due to direct pressure on the windpipe or by irritation of the nerve which leads to muscles of the throat. Heart failure can also lead to shortness of breath and cough.

6. **Bronchitis :-** Bronchitis is very common especially in winter and is caused by a bacterial or a viral infection and so the inflammation of bronchial tubes is called Bronchitis. Cough is always associated with bronchitis which could by repeated and dry or productive with sputum.

7. **Whooping Cough :-** This is an infectious disease caused by a specific germ known as ***Bordetella pertusis***. It is most common in childhood and most children are now vaccinated against it. This cough is typical and easily recognized – the child coughs several times in such quick succession that there is not the time to draw the breath between them, he becomes blue in the face, the veins of the forehead and scalp stand out, the eyes become prominent and the tongue is often protruded. At last when the child appears about to suffocate, the air is suddenly breathed in with a loud whooping noise. This may be followed by a second or series of coughs or whoops before the bout is over.

8. **Cough associated with Bronchial Asthma :-** Bronchial Asthma is an allergic disorder of respiratory tract manifested by episodic, marked spasm and narrowing of bronchi leading to respiratory distress, wheezing and dry cough.

# 2
# How Your Body Fights Illness

Lungs are situated in the chest and perform vital activity of respiration. This is the process in which air passes in and out of the lungs to allow the blood to absorb oxygen and to give off carbon dioxide and water.

Nose and throat are equipped with an elaborate lymphatic system. Adenoids are situated at the back of the nose and the tonsils in the throat. Their purpose is to capture and destroy germs settling on the mucous membrane of the nose and throat and this they constantly do without showing any symptoms themselves.

When a large number of germs or an unusually virulent type of germ is captured by these masses of lymphatic tissue, a brisk battle results, accompanied by the symptoms of inflammation – known as TONSILLITIS.

Neighbouring glands in the neck may be involved as reinforcements, and they in their turn become inflammed. Eventually the tonsils and glands will overcome the infection, and the inflammation will subside. This may occur without permanent damage to the tonsils, in which case they will live to fight another day. But sometimes the tonsils are so severely damaged by the infection that they can not adequately resist subsequent infection. In this case the next invading germ makes its home in the weakened tonsils and we thus have septic tonsils, source of constant infection and ill health. The same is true of adenoids and of tissues throughout the body.

Enlargement and disease of the adenoids results in breathing through the mouth, frequent colds, deafness through blocking of the Eustachian tube in the ear. It also causes chronic bronchitis, sometimes loss of appetite, chronic ill health and dulling of intelligence.

An attack of acute tonsillitis is accompanied by a high temperature and great feeling of unwellness. Tonsils are large, red and painful and may be covered by a coating of yellow matter and the membrane seen in diphtheria. During an attack swallowing of solid food will be impossible and the patient may be confined to bed and given plenty of fluid to drink. Gargles of salt and water are sometimes very helpful. A gargle of cider vinegar and water is most effective. A drink of honey and cider vinegar is very good. The honey is an energizer and the cider vinegar, a natural antiseptic. Enlarged tonsils and adenoids are a sure sign that a person is suffering from a very toxic condition affecting these organs and only change of dietary habit will promote health and vitality and render him that immunity necessary to fight off these infections.

The adenoids are growths of the lymphatic on the back of the upper part of the throat into which the nose opens (similar in structure to the tonsils ). Very often when a cold develops or there is an acute infection of the upper respiratory tract these growths or adenoids get very swollen, sometimes fill up the portion of the throat and obstruct the passage of air through the nose and into the Eustachian tubes.

To be on the safe side when the fever is high a doctor should be consulted.

## PATHOGENIC MICRO-ORGANISMS

Infections of the respiratory tract can be considered as infections of the upper and lower respiratory tract.

However, the division is not clear cut, since in lower respiratory tract infections, there may be some degree of involvement of the upper respiratory tract and the organisms causing infection may be identical in both. However, in the lower respiratory tract, the bronchi and alveoli of the lungs are included which are virtually sterile, while the upper respiratory tract (nose, throat, sinuses) contain pathogenic; eg; ***Staphylococci*** and haemolytic ***Streptococci*** in the nose and frequently in the nasopharynx.

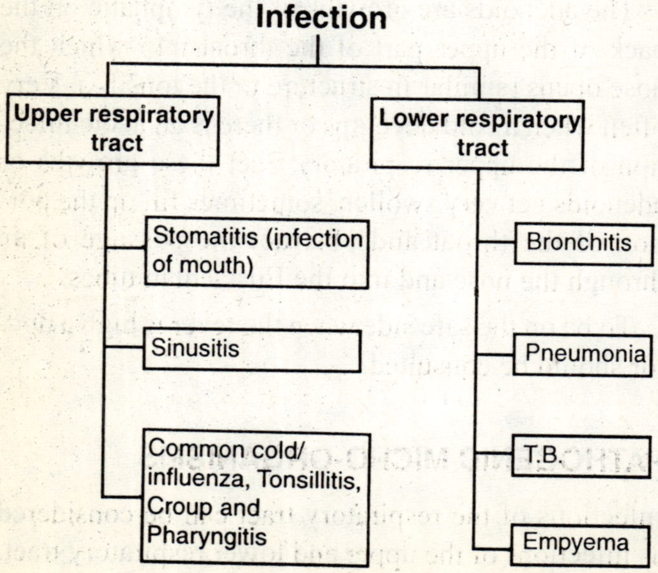

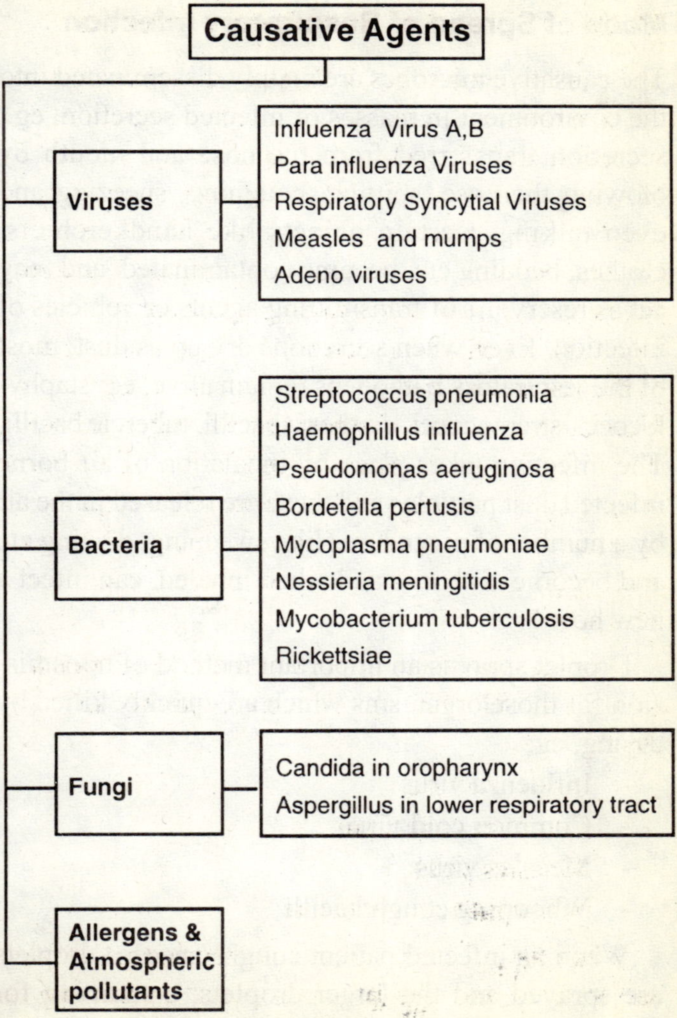
Causative Agents
Viruses
Influenza Virus A,B
Para influenza Viruses
Respiratory Syncytial Viruses
Measles and mumps
Adeno viruses
Bacteria
Streptococcus pneumonia
Haemophillus influenza
Pseudomonas aeruginosa
Bordetella pertusis
Mycoplasma pneumoniae
Nessieria meningitidis
Mycobacterium tuberculosis
Rickettsiae
Fungi
Candida in oropharynx
Aspergillus in lower respiratory tract
Allergens &
Atmospheric
pollutants

## Mode of Spread of Respiratory infection

The causative microbes are mainly disseminated into the environment in masses of infected secretion, eg., secretion transferred from the nose and mouth by blowing the nose, spitting, coughing, sneezing and even talking. Certain objects like handkerchiefs, clothes, bedding etc. become contaminated and may act as reservoirs of transmitting agents or vehicles of infection. Even when secretions dry up as dust, most of the respiratory pathogens remain alive, eg; staphylococci, streptococci, diptheria bacilli, tubercle bacilli. The infection takes place by inhalation of air borne infected dust particles and these are released in the air by a number of procedures like sweeping, dusting etc and become air borne and when inhaled, can infect a new host.

Droplet spray is an important method of transmission for those organisms which are quickly killed by drying, eg;

- Influenza virus
- Common cold virus
- Measles virus
- Whooping cough bacilli

When an infected patient coughs/sneezes droplets are sprayed and the larger droplets, containing for example bacteria such as ***N. meningitidis*** or Haemolytic streptococci, settle down on the ground, but it is the smaller droplets, containing for example T.B. bacilli which become air borne and are inhaled by people in close contact. Therefore, respiratory infections spread rapidly in communities where over crowding can not be avoided.

# 3
# Prevention from Common Cold and Cough

General prevention can markedly reduce chances of catching common cold and other respiratory problems. Common cold is a catarrhal disorder of the upper respiratory tract, which may be viral or an allergic reaction, and marked by acute coryza, slight rise in body temperature, chilly sensations, general indisposition and bodyache. It usually gets complicated due to super added secondary bacterial infection.

Common cold is an infectious disease. The intensity of cold depends largely upon the harmfulness of the germs and to the degree of susceptibility of the individual. It is common experience that some people are much more liable to catch cold than others. Therefore, people with cold should treat themselves as infectious and keep out of crowded places, refrain from visiting sick persons and if they must go whilst in the streaming stages, be careful to cover the mouth and nose with a handkerchief when sneezing or coughing.

Precautions to prevent catching of colds by people when they have been with a person who has a cold or when cold is epidemic such as;

1. Spraying the rooms with disinfectants.
2. Burning material which yield disinfectant vapours.
3. Putting eucalyptus oil on handkerchief.
4. A routine of spraying and gargling does help in warding off colds.
5. A healthy mode of life and fresh air in the house without draughts are really the best preventives.
6. Sudden exposure to cold atmosphere or cold water should be avoided.
7. Avoid rugs.
8. Protection from soil, dust and abnoxious smelling substances.

The teeth, throat and nose should be examined if the tendency to catch cold is very frequent.

Common colds get complicated due to super added secondary bacterial infection when cough manifests itself.

# 4

# Non-Medicinal Care

## ACUPRESSURE

According to Gach where there are tension and stress, aches and pains, menstrual cramps, arthritis or asthma; acupressure is a treatment of choice. The same holds good for general preventive health care, fighting cold, improving muscles tone or boosting energy level.

The word chi denotes body's vital life force. Acupressurists believe that soreness surrounding a point indicates blockage of chi. Stimulations of the point release the chi, so the soreness will go away. It does not held in diseases clearly caused by bacteria like acute high fevers and contagious diseases. Why and how acupressure works is debatable says Dr. Warfield.

But studies have shown that manipulating points works to release endorphins and enkephalins- the bodies' naturals narcotics. Proponents say cold - mitten friction is good for peoples who suffer an inordinate number of colds for those lacking energy. Anything that stimulates your immune system is going to increase your ability to fight infections.

## AROMA-THERAPY

1. Aroma is fragrance and the pleasant smell means aroma.
2. The aromatic oils are used as edible oils also; like menthol oil which is carminative and good for digestion.
3. Aromatic oil like clove oil for tooth ache (medicinal property) which is given as counter irritation and as an antiseptic and antimicrobial activity – absorption through the skin.
4. Our concentration is on the herbs and their essential oils, which are therapeutically beneficial for common cold and cough. The most common and known herbs for this is mentha herb oil, eucalyptus oil. But in this research we have identified different plants and we have tried our best effort to establish its therapeutical activity and identifying its principal constituents.

# 5

# 101 Simple Herbal Remedies

## (i) HOME REMEDIES

Home remedies denote easily available and accessible materials around us, which are commonly used to under take the care of the ailing person. This chapter is meant to provide basic information about the assessment of the materials available in the house to treat the ailing person suffering from cough and common cold. This would provide knowledge to use materials off hand and to give relief to the suffering patient with immediate effect. Most of the time these remedies will be found absolutely curative and for acute problems the remedy would act as first aid to the patient.

1. Boil one teaspoon of fenugreek (Methi) seeds in a cup of water, add a teaspoon of tea leaves and honey. This preparation is a good remedy for cold, cough, sore throat and fever. Lemon and honey in hot water, tea and coffee are effective in suppressing the cough reflex.
2. Steam inhalation for grown up people is an effective and safe remedy. Menthol crystals or eucalyptus oil or Eu de cologne etc., can be added to hot water producing steam for inhalation. It reduces cough and also makes it easier to bring up phlegm. For inhalation put a towel over the head which has been held just above the water, and encourage him to inhale deeply for 3 to 4 minutes. This treatment may be undertaken any time as may be necessary but preferably before going to bed. Infants should not be given inhalation. It is desirable that a baby should be laid on its side without a pillow to avoid the mucus running down the back of its throat. This may make breathing slightly easier. Olive oil or mustard oil (warm) may be applied (gentle massage) to the chest, as and when necessary but preferably at night which act as decongestant. A drop or two of Olive oil or mustard oil is applied by finger to the nostrils for some relief. The aforesaid methods of massage and application of oil to nostrils would help to clear the catarrh and the nose.

3. A powder of dried ginger, black pepper and long pepper in equal quantities can be taken with honey thrice a day for good relief in dry cough.
4. Tulsi is a useful herb for the cough, cold and croup in children. The warm juice of tulsi leaves mixed with juice of onion and ginger with honey in equal parts is recommended.
5. Powdered pepper mixed with a little honey and pure ghee taken in small quantities in a cup of hot milk at night, for relieving cough, cold and sore throat.
6. Black pepper powder (1/4 tsp.) is mixed with equal quantities of powder of caraway seeds and a pinch of common salt. This mixture can be taken frequently with hot water for dry cough and throat irritation.
7. The juices of ginger, lemon & onion mixed in equal quantities. One tbsp. can be taken frequently for relief in cold.
8. Garlic has an antibiotic property. Two raw cloves can be used twice a day at a first sign of cold and will be continued for the duration of the cold.
9. The paste of one segment of bulbs of garlic boiled in water with five to ten grams of sugar can be taken twice a day for relief in cold.

10. Ginger is an excellent remedy for cough and cold. Ginger tea can be prepared by adding bits of ginger into boiled water before adding tea leaves is an effective remedy.
11. Ginger can also be used with honey; 10 ml. of ginger juice mixed with 10 gm. of honey can be taken before meals for dry cough and also in whooping cough.
12. One gram of powdered black pepper with ghee sugar and honey in equal quantities is a good remedy for cough.
13. A mixture of finely powdered black pepper, cinnamon, black cumin and cardamom seeds in equal quantities can be taken with a cup of sweet milk is also another good remedy for cold as well as cough.
14. Boil 5 black pepper with 1 pinch of salt for 15 minutes and strain. The decoction is effective for cold and can be taken twice a day.
15. Fried turmeric (1 to 2 gms.) can be taken with honey thrice a day. This would bring relief from cough and cold.
16. To get rid of congestion due to cold, put a teaspoon of turmeric powder into a panful of steaming hot water. Inhale vapours for a few minutes to relieve congestion.

17. Turmeric is also an effective remedy for developing immune system. A teaspoonful of powder or paste should be added to a cup of warm milk and taken with sugar thrice a day. This strengthens immune system, prevents lungs complications and is good for influenza.
18. Turmeric can also be used in bronchitis. Simplest treatment of bronchitis is the administration of one teaspoon full of turmeric powder thrice daily.
19. For a blocked nose, gently apply in and out of nostrils few drops of mustard oil, this helps to open blocked nose and eases breathing.
20. Long pepper powder (half a teaspoonful) mixed with two spoonful of honey and half a teaspoonful of ginger juice administered thrice a day would effectively counteract the onset of influenza and cold.
21. Boil some crushed garlic in water and use it for gargling will reduce swelling of the throat due to cough.
22. For sore throat and Hoarseness of voice, keep a peppercorn or two in the throat. They greatly soothe the throat and gives relief in sore throat and cough.

23. Extract the juice of fresh Tulsi leaves and bel flowers, take one teaspoonful twice a day for cough & cold.
24. Boil six tablespoon of wheat bran (Choakar) in 300 ml of water, add salt or sugar to taste and taken as hot drink. This preparation is a good remedy for cough.
25. Boil half cup of vermicelli, laung - 2 pc, dry ginger - ½ pc, in one glass of water, add sugar and salt to taste. As a hot drink it is useful remedy for cough & cold.
26. Fry makhana (two cups) and gum accacia (gond) - 2 tablespoon, separately in pure ghee. Grind the fried gum with poppy seeds (khas khash) - 3 tablespoon, vitis nucifera (munnakka) - 24 pc, coconut - ¼ pc, almonds - 12 seeds, dry ginger (sonth) - 2 or 3 pc, ajowain - 1 pinch and cardamom (choti elaichi) - 4 or 6 pcs. The above grinded material is to be fried and then boiled in water with makhana. Sprinkle sonth and ajowain powder over the extract obtained and taken for cold, all types of cough and sore throat.

## (ii) SINGLE HERBAL REMEDIES

1. Decoction of liquorice root (Mulethi) should be given with sugar or honey as a vehicle to clear the phlegm and thus give relief in severe cough.
2. The liquorice root (Mulethi) is backed or kept in a microwave oven or under the ash of wood coke till it becomes soft. It can be taken twice or thrice in a day, taking in saliva by chewing is a good remedy, for cough and sore throat, which work as a lozenge.
3. Twelve grams of Banafsha flowers (Viola odorata) boiled in 50 ml. of milk, it is good to sieve the milk before taking is a useful remedy for dry cough.
4. Sipping nector of Bansa (Adhatoda vasica) fresh flowers or decoction of its leaves is good for sore throat, dry cough and it is also a good expectorant.
5. Decoction of the bark of acacia (Babul tree) mixed with rock salt should be used for gargles gives relief in sore throat and Hoarseness of voice.
6. In case of running nose, smoke from burning roots of Amaltas or turmeric should be inhaled. It will encourage a copious discharge and would shortly provide relief.

# (iii) SIMPLE COMPOUND REMEDIES

1. Pomegranates (Punica granatum) outer covering 40 gms; kali mirch (Piper nigrum) 10 gm., Pipali (Piper longum) 6 gms are finely powdered. Thick consistency syrup is prepared from 80 gms of Gur. The finely powdered mixture is mixed with the Gur syrup. Tablets weighing 2 gms each are prepared after cooling the syrup. One tablet 4 times a day provides relief in cough & whooping cough.
2. Six gms. of garlic and an equal quantity of gur pounded together and may be given at bed time is a useful remedy for cold.
3. The powder of Yashti madhu (Mulethi), vacha (Acorus calamus) and Kulanjana (Alpinia galanga) made into a paste with honey should be used as linctus gives relief in dry cough and sore throat.
4. Lavang, Jaiphal, choti peepal (10 gms each), kali mirch-20 gms, Sonth-160 gms are finely powdered and mixed with 10 gms of Powdered Misri or Gur is an effective remedy for cough and fever due to cold.
5. A two grams pill made by mixing powder of Harar, Sonth, Nagarmotha and Gur is very useful in cough and cold.

6. Sonth, Yavasa, Kakrasinghi, Munakka, Kachur and Misri or Gur are taken in equal quantities and powdered. One to two gram powder can be taken with honey provide relief in cough.
7. For ordinary cough, mix lemon juice, honey and glycerine in equal quantities, taken one teaspoon full 3 to 4 times a day.
8. 10 gms powder of each of Piplamul, Pipali, Kalimirch and sonth can be taken with honey gives relief in cough, coryza and sore throat.
9. Vach, kulanjan, bakuchi and kattha are taken in equal parts, finely powdered and mixed with betel juice and small tablets are prepared. One tablet can be taken 3 to 4 times a day for cold and cough.
10. Mix ½ tsp. of ajowain seeds, 2 clove and pinch of salt, powdered and taken with honey gives relief in severe cold.
11. Boil 2 teaspoon of khaskhas (opium) seeds and 3 tsp. bits of liquorice root in one cup of water for 10 minutes. Strain and taken for dry cough.
12. Boil one tsp. each liquorice and cinnamon with one tablespoon of ginger paste in one cup of water for 10 minutes. Strain adds honey and taken for severe cough, sore throat and Hoarseness of voice.

13. Mix 1 tsp. of turmeric powder along with ¼ tsp. ajowain powder in three teacup of hot water. Allow to cool. Take 1-2 tsp. of this decoction along with 1 tsp. of honey twice daily for cold, cough and nasal congestion.
14. Prepare a tea of ½ tsp. ginger with ¼ tsp. of cinnamon & cloves each per cup of water. Sweeten with honey and taken for cough.
15. A lozenge made by mixing one part of Guggal, nine part mulethi powder and one part black pepper is beneficial for cough.
16. Decoction of equal quantities of Pushkar mool, kaiphal, bharangi, sonth & pipali is used for cough and other respiratory ailments.
17. Kaiphal, motha, bharangi bark, dhania, pittapapara, vacha, harar, kakrasinghi, deodar burada, sonth each weighing 5 gms. One tsp. can be taken with a cup of hot milk for cold and cough.
18. Boil one gram each of bansa, sonth, giloe, daruhaldi, lal chandan, chitrak, neembark, kutki, patol patra, triphala, kutaj bark in a cup of water and 1 tsp. can be taken gives relief in whooping cough.
19. Powdered 5 gm each of Giloe, Neembark,

Motha, Indrajaue, Sonth, Lal Chandan and Pipal, taken 1 tsp. with honey is an effective remedy for cold.

20. Boil 10 gms each of Kataili small, Sonth, Giloe & Pushkar mool in two cup of water, one teaspoon full can be taken twice a day for sore throat, & clear phlegm thus gives relief in cough.
21. Decoction of Khireti, choti kateli, badi kateli, and munakka in equal quantities mixed with honey is useful for pitta cough.
22. Amla, Puid khajoor, kakoli, pippali and kalimirch in equal parts are powdered and mixed with ghee and honey is a good remedy for cough and asthma.
23. Puid khajoor, peepal, munakka, misri and dhan ki lai, (in equal quantities) are powdered and mixed with ghee and honey and taken 5-10 gm twice daily for cough.
24. Decoction of kaiphal, rohish ghas, bharangi, nagarmotha, dhania, vach, badi harar, kakrsinghi, pitpapra, sonth & deodaru is mixed with honey and powdered fried heeng for whooping cough, expel phlegm.
25. Equal quantities of pippali, padmakh, munakka,

ripe fruits of big kataili are powdered and mixed with ghee ad honey. It is useful for cough and asthma.

## (iv) COMPLEX COMPOUND REMEDIES

1. Panchang of Kataili small (5 gm) & 100 bits of kataili big are soaked overnight in 1 litre of water and then boiled. The decoction is mixed with Gur or Honey to form the syrup, add Dalchini powder, Nagkesar and Trikuta in equal quantities, one teaspoonful should be taken twice a day for chronic cough.
2. Talispatra, Ajowain, Amalbael, Trikatu (Sonth, pippali and kali mirch) taken in equal parts and mixed with one-fourth trisugandhi (Dalchini, Tejpat, Elaichi) and twice the amount of Gur. This is a good remedy for cough and asthma.

## (v) GENERIC REMEDIES

1. The following prescriptions are recommended for cold and cough.
   - (i) Vasa churna, 2 gm; Shukti Bhasma, 125 mg; Trikuti churna, 1 gm (to be taken thrice daily)
   - (ii) Old Gur, 10 gm & Mustard oil 10 gm; to be taken in cold weather (Recommended by Acharya charkrapani)

(iii) Bharangi, 2 gms; Nagarmotha, 2 gms (should be ground into paste with water and taken twice daily with warm water.)

2. In fever accompanied by cough, two tablets of Tribhuvana kirti ras, a teaspoonful of ginger juice and honey should be given 3 to 4 times a day.

3. A paste of equal parts of raisins, dates, black pepper, vidhanga, bahera, long pepper and honey should be use to get relief in cough.

4. Standard Ayurvedic preparations, Rasa Sindur (120 mgs) and pravala pisthis (240 mg) to be taken thrice daily with ghee for acute & chronic cough and bronchitis.

5. Khadiradi vati : Kattha (*Accacia catechu*), javitri (*Myristica fragrans*), kali mirch (*Piper nigrum*) and supari (*Areca catechu*). The tablet should be sucked as lozenge five times a day for cough, congested throat accompanies bronchitis. The main ingredient catechu helps to relieve congestion.

6. Sitopaladi churna : Banslochan; Pippali (*Piper longum*); choti elaichi seeds (*Elettaria cardamom*) and Dalchini (*Cinnamomum zeylanicum*), should be taken three or four times a day with honey for dry cough.

7. Kaphagni vati: Kapoor (*Cinnamomum camphora*); Kasturi; Lavang (*Syzgium aromaticum*); Peepal (*Piper longum*); Bahera (*Terminalia bellirica*); Kulanjan (Alpinia galanga) and rind of Anar (*Punica granatum*). One tablet should be taken three times a day for whooping & dry cough.

8. Vyoshadya vati: Talispatra (*Taxus buccata*); Zeera (*Cuminum cyminum*); Peepal (*Piper longum*); chavya (*Piper cubeba*); Sonth (*Zingiber officinale*); Kali Mirch (*Piper nigrum*); Amalvet (*Rheum emodi*), Chitrak (*Plumbago zeylanica*) and Imli (*Tamarindus indica*). The tablets should be sucked as lozenge two to three times a day for cough and cold with sore throat.

9. The decoction of Rasna (*Pluchea* sp.); Kharenṭi (*Sida cordifolia*); Trikatu (kali mirch — *Piper nigrum*, pippali—*Piper longum*, adrak (Sonth)—*Zingiber officinale*; Kantakari (*Solanum xanthocarpum*) and Gokhru (*Tribulus terristris*) mixed with Ghee is an effective remedy for all types of cough.

10. Drugs administered in common cough and whooping cough may also provide some relief

in cases of asthma. Bronchial asthma is supposed to originate from afflictions of the stomach and gastrointestinal tract. Hence patient complains of indigestion, consptipation or diarrhoea. In Ayurveda standard preparations for these complaints are (I) Chyavanprasha & (ii) Agastiya Rasayana.

11. Dashmuli Ghrita, Kantakayavleh and Panchmuli Kashaya can be used for whooping cough.

12. Hoarseness results from laryngitis, the treatment consist of Eladi vati, 2 or three tablets can be taken twice a day that should be sucked as lozenge. Powder of Mulethi and Vacha should also be given thrice a day with honey.

13. For chronic cough & coryza, the effective remedies are;

    (i) Mahalaxmi vilas – (120 mg to be taken with powder of mulethi, honey and ghee).

    (ii) Chitrak Hiratiki – (10 gm to be taken in the morning and at night with warm cows milk).

    (iii) Madhuyasthyadi Quath – (50 ml, can be used thrice daily)

14. Some other standard Ayurvedic preparations for cough are;

(i) Chaturshana Churna – can be taken twice a day with warm water.

(ii) Eladi Churana – thrice a day with warm water or honey.

(iii) Aparajita Leha – Two times daily for whooping cough.

15. Kaphachintamani – 120 mg can be taken thrice daily for cough & bronchitis.
16. Kaphaketu – 120 mg to be taken for cold and cough.
17. Shringyadi churna – 2 gm can be used with warm water 3 times a day for cough & whooping cough & bronchitis.
18. Swasha Kasa – Chintamani Ras, Survarna-Pushpasuga Ras and Kankasava is recommended in cases of asthma, bronchial asthma and in chronic coughs.
19. Shwasari lavan- 500 mg with honey can be taken 2 or 3 times a day for cough and bronchitis.
20. Gajanand vati – 200 mg tablet taken 2 times a day with fresh water for cold & cough.
21. Sanjivani vati – one tablet can be taken thrice a day with warm milk for whooping cough and asthma.

22. Vasa – Kushmand Khand – 10-20 gm can be used 2 times a day with warm goat milk for all types of cough.
23. Extract 1 tsp. each juice from fresh ginger, betel leaf and tulsi leavs. Add 1 tsp. honey. Take 2 or 3 times a day for cold & cough.
24. Mix equal quantities of the juice of lime, ginger and onion. Take 2 tsp. twice a day for cold.
25. Grind ½ tsp. saffron in milk and apply on nose, head and cheeks etc. for cold and Phlegm.
26. Grind 2 tsp. tail pepper, 1 tsp. each dried ginger, camphor and asafoetida either with an adequate quantity of rose water or milk into a smooth pest and apply on chest in congestion due to cold.
27. Add 1 – 3 drops saunf oil to 1 tbsp. Honey. Take a teaspoon at a time for cough.
28. Add 2 – 3 drops of almond oil to pomegranate juice and taken for dry cough.
29. Add 1 or 2 drops of almond oil to a glass of milk and taken for dry cough and cough due to heat.
30. Heat 1 tsp. garlic juice in 3 tbsp. gingelly oil. Rub this preparation on the chest and throat to expel phlegm.

31. Crush 2 tsp. ajowain seeds. Mix in a glass of buttermilk and taken to reduce blockage due to dried phlegm.
32. Chandramrita, yavakshara and talishadi mixed with syrup of Lisora can be used for congestion of chest.

Consult a doctor when;

1. Coughing persists after a common cold has cleared up.
2. Coughing produces yellow or green spit. This may means child has developed bronchitis.
3. Coughing is accompanied with pain and shortness of breath.
4. Coughing occurs in spasms.
5. Child appears to be generally unwell.

# Appendix I

## Single Herbs

1. Bansa *(Adhatoda vasica)*
2. Kateli *(Solanum xanthocarpum)*
3. Kuth *(Saussurea lappa)*
4. Tulsi *(Ocimum sanctum)*
5. Mulethi *(Glycyrrhiza glabra)*
6. Pippali *(Piper longum)*
7. Sonth *(Zingiber officinale)*
8. Kali Mirch *(Piper nigrum)*

## Antiallergic and anti-inflammatory drugs

1. Kali Mirch *(Piper nigrum)*
2. Haldi *(Curcuma longa)*

3. Giloe *(Tinospora cordifolia)*
4. Kuth *(Saussurea lappa)*
5. Punarnava *(Boehravia diffusa)*
6. Harar *(Terminalia chebula)*
7. Nisoth *(Operculina turpethum)*

## Herbal Compound Uneful in Respiratory Ailments

1. Brahma rasayan
2. Nagabala rasayan
3. Pippalivardhamana rasayan
4. Ajamamsa rasayan
5. Dashmoola rasayan
6. Pankajakastoori rasayan
7. Dehaposhakaymakam
8. Amrit preasha ghritam

Used for longer period to achieve acquired immunity of respiratory system

# Appendix II

**A brief poster presentation is being made of Linctus 'H' highlighting the scientific evaluation and its preparation, which is an international way to assess a medicinal preparation.**

# TITLE

Linctus 'H' prepared by authenticated sterile herbs proved effective and safe on studying in vivo, in vitro and toxicity parameters.

Poster produced by
**Dr. S. FAROOQ**
M.Sc., Ph.D. (Gold Medalist), D.Sc., F.R.S.H. (London)
321-D, Okhla Village, New Delhi-110025 (India)

# TITLE

# Introduction

Plant is a nature designed compound. Diverse ingredients are present in a plant e.g.; Oligosaccharides, EFA, Bitters, Anthocyanins, Alkaloids, Mucilage etc. Which form a semblance of useful remedial substance on holistic pattern. Traditional texts with commentaries on safe usage of herbs, in vivo studies have been enshrined in Vedas since the time immemorial. (Vedas are Indian Health science textbooks, 5000 years old). Phytomedicines based on HOLISTIC approach using ingredients as a whole, which is a natural combination of all constituents, are safe, efficacious and beneficent and this fact is also authenticated by researchers' scientific data. Considering the above facts and keeping in view the aspects of wholesome use of ingredients a medicine was designed and tested for efficacy with instant relief for 'LARYNGITIS' it was named as LINCTUS 'H'. 'H' stands for HOLISTIC.

Herbs selected were authenticated not merely with the conventional organoleptic testing practice for the standardization and potency testing, but here the herbs used were evaluated as per the monographs and the specifications given in I.P. and B.P. using latest testing equipment and techniques available such as spectrophotometry, chromatography, analytical and quantitative tests, macro and micro studies etc. After preparing the product which was having all clinical references in traditional text books it was passed through minutest scrutiny of in vitro, in vivo, pharmacokinetic, pharmacodynamic and Toxicological studies in human and animal models to confirm the efficacy of the product as per the OECD and FDA guidelines.

## ETHNOBOTANICAL DATA

* Piper nigrum
* Piper longum
* Zingiber officinale

The fourth ingredient is honey which, is a vehicle, preservative and is the base to prepare the 'Linctus–H'. So its identification is also to be ascertained.

# PIPER NIGRUM

| | | |
|---|---|---|
| HINDI NAME | : | Maricha |
| ENGLISH NAME | : | Black Pepper |
| TEXTBOOK REFERENCES | : | British Herbal Pharmacopoeia |

## MACROSCOPIC STUDY

| | | |
|---|---|---|
| PART USED | : | Seeds |
| SHAPE | : | Rounded |
| SURFACE | : | Rough |
| COLOUR | : | Black |
| COLOUR ON BREAKING | : | Off White |
| ODOUR | : | Characteristic |
| TASTE | : | Trenchant and Biting |

## MICROSCOPIC STUDY

1. Group of stone cells are visible with intercellular space the

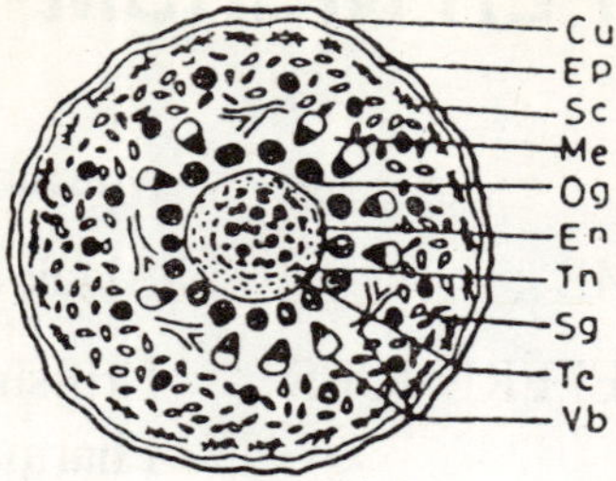


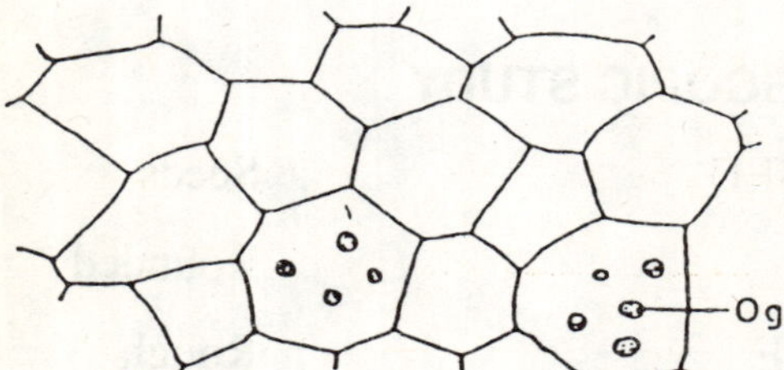


2

**Fig.** Parenchymatous Mesocarp posses oil globules.

| | | |
|---|---|---|
| DUST PARTICLES | : | Not Present |

## CHEMICAL STUDY

| | | | |
|---|---|---|---|
| COLOUR | : | Black | |
| MOISTURE | : | Up to permissible limit | |
| FOREIGN MATTER | : | Not present | |
| CHEMICAL CONSTITUENTS | : | Range | Observation |
| Volatile Oil | : | 1-2.5% | 2% |
| Alkaloids | : | 5-9% | 8% |
| Piperine | : | 2-5% | 3% |

## Result

This ingredient is as per the reference of Indian Pharmacopoeia and British Herbal Pharmacopoeia and suitable for manufacturing of herbal medicine.

# PIPER LONGUM

| | | |
|---|---|---|
| HINDI NAME | : | PEEPALI |
| ENGLISH NAME | : | Long Pepper |
| TEXTBOOK REFERENCE | : | British Herbal Pharmacopoeia |

## MACRO SCOPIC STUDY

| | | |
|---|---|---|
| ENGLISH NAME | : | Black Pepper |
| PART USED | : | Fruit |
| SHAPE | : | Cylindrical with rounded ends |
| SURFACE | : | Rough |
| COLOUR | : | Blackish |
| COLOUR ON BREAKING | : | Dark Green |
| ODOUR | : | Aromatic |
| TASTE | : | Trenchant and Biting |

## MICROSCOPIC STUDY

Some stone cells (from endocarp) appear as row c 'beaker' shaped thick walled.

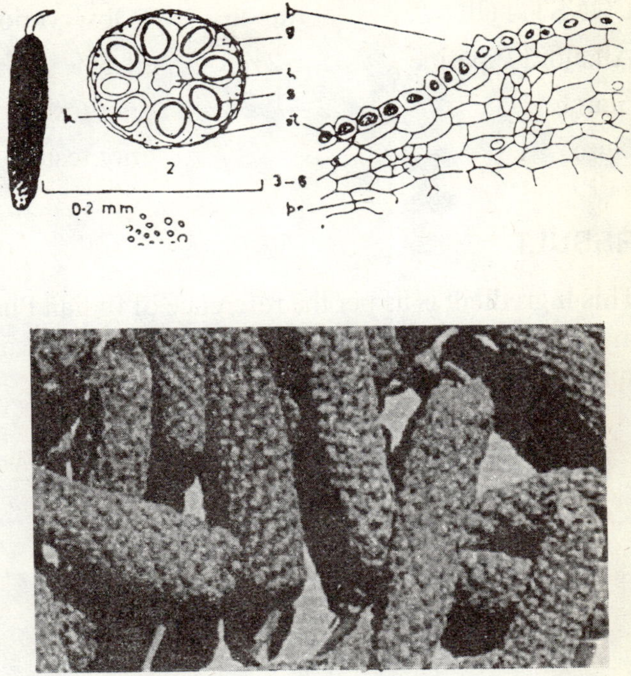


**Fig.** Peepali fruits and their T.S.

DUST PARTICLES : Not present

## CHEMICAL STUDY

MOISTURE : Up to the permissible limit

FOREIGN MATTER : Not Present

| CHEMICAL CONSTITUENTS | : Range | Observation |
|---|---|---|
| Alkaloid Piperine | : 1-2% | 1.5% |
| Starch | : — | not tested |
| Gum | : — | not tested |

## RESULT

This ingredient is as per the reference of Indian Pharmacopoeia and British Herbal Pharmacopoeia and suitable for manufacturing herbal medicine.

# ZINGIBER OFFICINALE

| | | |
|---|---|---|
| HINDI NAME | : | Sunthi |
| ENGLISH NAME | : | Dry Ginger |
| TEXTBOOK REFERENCES | : | British Herbal Pharmacopoeia |

## MACROSCOPIC STUDY

| | | |
|---|---|---|
| PART USED | : | Rhizome |
| SHAPE | : | Irregular Branched |
| SURFACE | : | Rough |
| COLOUR | : | Light Brown |
| COLOUR ON BREAKING | : | Buffy Brown |
| ODOUR | : | Characteristic |
| TASTE | : | Ginger like |

## MICROSCOPIC STUDY

Cork, Cortex, endosperm and ground tissues are clearly visible.

DUST PARTICLES : Not Present

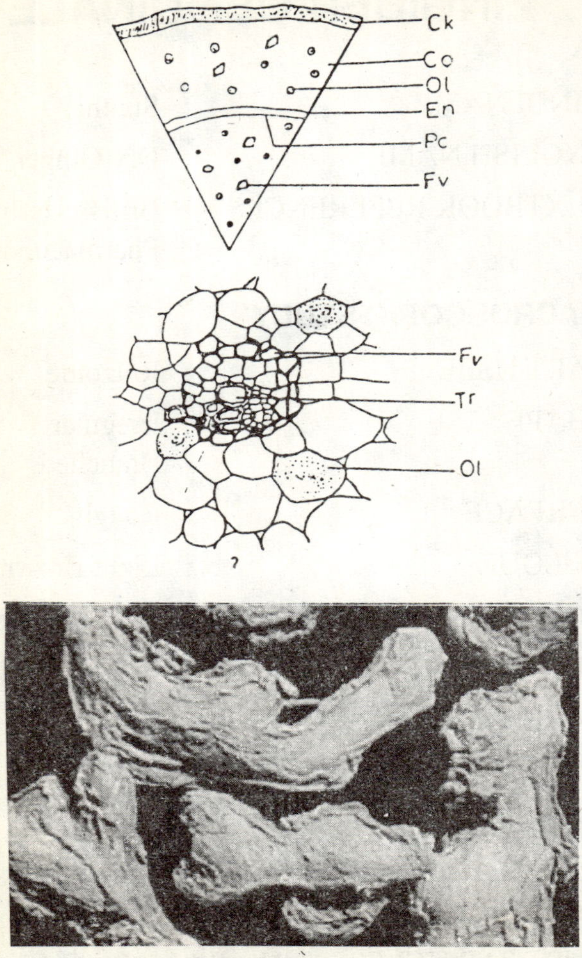


**Fig.** Ginger Rhizome and their T.S. showing cork, cortex, endosperm and ground tissue.

## CHEMICAL STUDY

| | | |
|---|---|---|
| MOISTURE | : Up to the permissible limit | |
| FOREIGN MATTER | : Not Present | |
| MOISTURE | : Up to permissible limit | |
| FOREIGN MATTER | : Not present | |
| CHEMICAL CONSTITUENTS | : Range | Observation |
| Oleoresin | : 5.3-8.6% | 7% |
| Volatile oil | : 1.5-2.2% | 2% |
| Lipids | : 6-8% | Not Tested |
| Proteins | : 10% | Not Tested |
| Starch | : 40-60% | Not Tested |

## Result

The ingredient is as per the reference of Indian Pharmacopoeia and British Herbal Pharmacopoeia and suitable for manufacturing herbal medicine.

# HONEY

| | | |
|---|---|---|
| HINDI NAME | : | Madhu |
| BOTANICAL NAME | : | Mel. (Honey) |
| TEXTBOOK REFERENCE | : | The Indian Materia Medica |

## MACRO SCOPIC STUDY

| | | |
|---|---|---|
| NATURE | : | Viscous/translucent liquid |
| COLOUR | : | Yellow to dark Brown |
| ODOUR | : | Agreeable |
| TASTE | : | Sweet |

## CHEMICAL ANALYSIS

| CHEMICAL CONSTITUENTS | : | RANGE |
|---|---|---|
| Carbohydrates (Invert Sugars) | : | 70-80% |
| Sucrose | : | 0.1-10% |

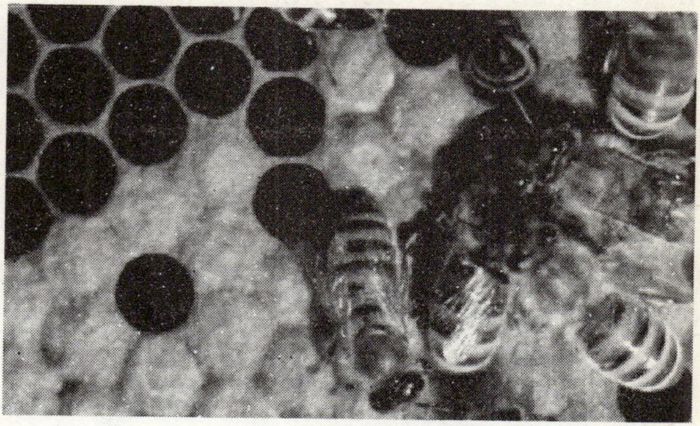

Fig. Honey hive.

## TEST FOR PURITY

10 ml of honey is shaken thoroughly with 5 ml of ether till they are miscible and later separate on standing. The upper ethereal layer is evaporated to dryness in porcelain dish. In natural honey, a transient red colouration is obtained on addition of 1 drop of 1% resorcinol HCl while in artificial invert sugar red colouration persists for some time.

### Refining of Honey

For 3000 parts of fresh honey take 875 parts of water 150 parts of washed, dried and pulverized charcoal, 70 parts of powdered chalk, and the white of 3 eggs beaten in 90 parts of water. Put the honey and the chalk in a vessel capable of containing 1/3 more than the mixture and boil for 3 minutes; then introduce the charcoal and stir up the whole. Add the whites of the eggs while continuing to stir and boil again for 3 minutes. Take from the fire and after allowing the liquid to cool for a quarter of an hour. Filter and to secure a perfectly clear liquid refilter on flannel.

# MANUFACTURING CHART

Manufacturing starts from procurement of fresh ingredients, which are first washed, cleaned and then treated for disinfection and then dried at a suitable temperature and subjected to the following steps.

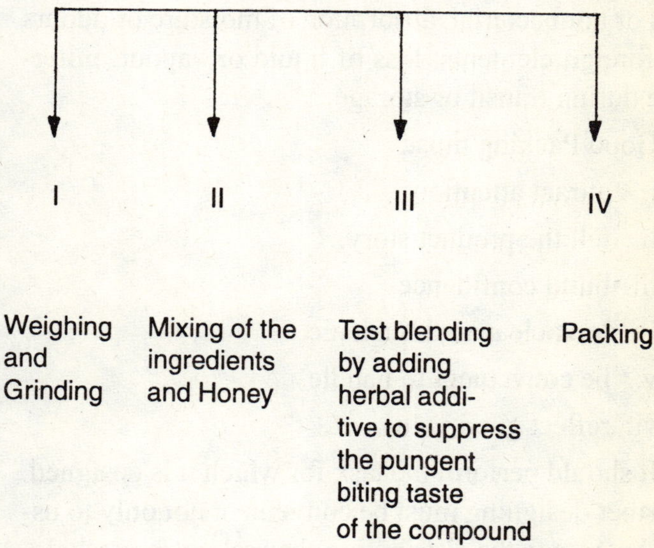

# PACKING

It is meant for protection, appeal, performance, convenience and cost effectiveness.

Hazards are breakage due to mechanical or manual handling during transportation, extremes of climatic conditions (melting, freezing), contamination- bacterial or nonbacterial, absorption of moisture or odours of foreign elements, loss of liquid or vapour, pilferage during transit or storage.

Good Packing must;

i. attract attention.

ii. tell the product story.

iii. build confidence.

iv. look clean and hygienic.

v. be convenient to handle.

vi. reflect good value.

It should perform the task for which it is designed. Further designing must be convenient not only to users but also to the distribution channels such as wholesalers and retailers.

i) Packing should be convenient to stock.

ii) Packing should be convenient to display.

iii) Packing should not waste shelf space.

iv) Retain its looks during the shelf life.

v) Master carbons are easy to dispose of.

vi) Cost effectiveness.

Considering the above facts a 100 ml glass jar with screw lid of pilfer proofing and sealing has been used.

# MICROBIOLOGICAL STUDY OF Linctus 'H'

## Determination of antimicrobial activity

The modified agar well diffusion method was used. Soyabean casein digest agar (SCDA) and Saboauraud Dextrose agar were used for bacterial and fungal cultures. The culture medium was inoculated with the microorganism suspended in soyabean digest-broth.

A total of 8 mm diameter wells were punched into the agar and filled with Linctus 'H'. Standard antibiotic was simultaneously used as positive control. The plates were incubated at 37°C for 18 hrs. The antimicrobial activity was evaluated by measuring the inhibition zone diameter observed.

**Table Antimicrobial activity of Linctus 'H'**

| S.No. | Sample | Antibacterial Activity | Antifungal Activity |
|---|---|---|---|
| 1 | Linctus 'H' | * 2+ | 2+ |

* 2+ = range of diameter of zone of inhibition is between 10-19 mm.

## Pharmacokinetics of the drugs

Pharmacokinetic studies involve kinetics of a drug and this refers to the modelling and mathematical description of the time course of disposition, i.e.; absorption, distribution, biotransformation and excretion of the drug in the whole animal.

## METABOLISM OR EXCRETION

.Studies on Absorption, Distribution, Metabolism and Excretion; are often referred to as:

### ADME

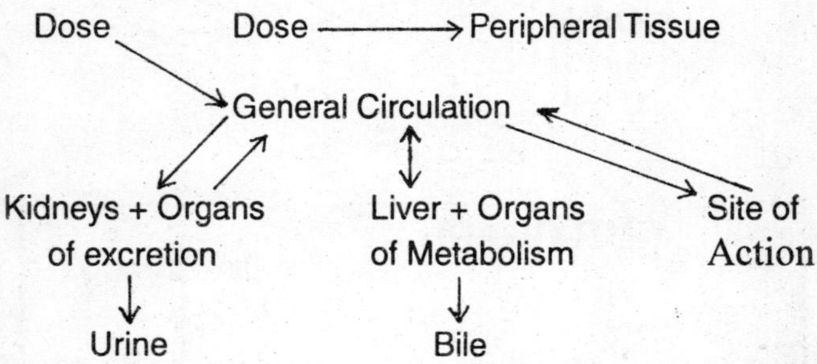


After completing 90 days toxicity study of 5 animals blood & excreta was kept under observation which remain normal and after completing the study these animals were dissected and organs were observed and were found in good shape which confirm its metabolism was not effected adversely.

# PHARMACODYNAMICS

Pharmacodynamics studies involve biochemical and physiological effects of drugs and the mechanism of their actions and effects of drugs with their chemical structure.

**Constituents** : Alkaloids and essential oil

Chemical Structures : NMR GRAPH

The compounds contained by Linctus-'H' affect mucosal cells and play an inhibiting role in controlling Laryngitis, improve blood circulation increases phagocytic action and detoxification process.

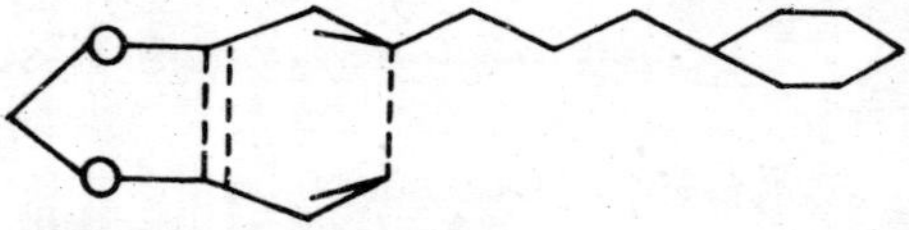

Piperine

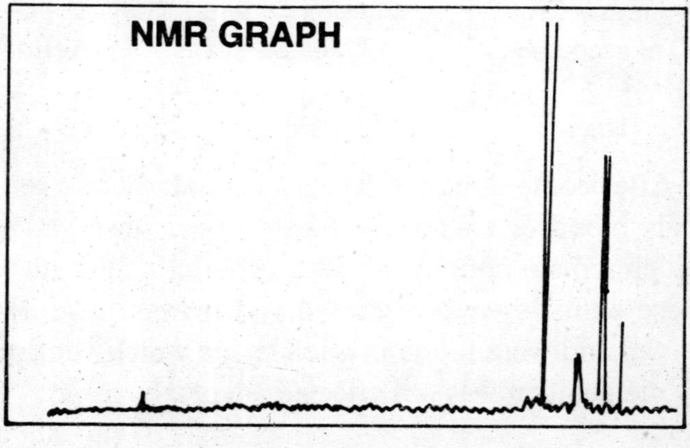

# TOXICITY

Toxicity denotes the degree of virulence of a toxic microbe or a poison. After establishing therapeutic efficacy subacute toxicity studies were carried out in albino rats and rhesus monkeys at a multiple doses of effective dose in compliance with F.D.A. and O.E.C.D. guidelines and Linctus 'H' compound was found safe and nontoxic even at very high doses, i.e.; 2 to 4 times of effective dose and additional advantages were evident by significant increase in haemoglobin and RBC count.

## BASIS OF IN VITRO STUDIES

# ANIMAL TOXICITY TESTS

## PROTOCOL OF TOXICITY STUDIES IN MONKEYS

1. Species : Rhesus
2. Number of Animals : 3 Males and 3 Females (Per dose group)
3. Duration : 90 Days
4. Route of Administration : Oral

5. Frequency of Administration : Daily
6. Doses : Effective Dose = 3.5 g/kg Body water

   Group I Control : Distilled water

   Group II Low Dose : 3.5 g/kg Body weight

   Group III Intermediate Dose : 7.0 g/kg Body weight

   Group IV High Dose : 14.0 g/kg Body weight
7. Parameters :
   1. Body Weight : Monthly
   2. Food Intake : Daily
   3. General Behavioural Tests : Daily
   4. Haematology : Monthly
   5. Urine Analysis : Monthly
   6. Biochemistry : Monthly
   7. Autopsy : At the end of 90 days

## PROTOCOL OF TOXICITY STUDIES IN RATS

1. Species : Charles Foster
2. Number of Animals (per dose group) : 15 males and 15 females

3. Duration : 90 days
4. Route of Administration : Oral
5. Frequency of Administration : Daily
6. Doses : Effective dose = 7 gm/kg

   Group I Control : Distilled water

   Group II Low dose : 7.0 g/kg body weight

   Group III Intermediate : 14.o g/kg body weight

   Group IV high dose : 28 g/kg body weight
7. Parameters
   1. Body weight : Monthly
   2. Haematological tests : Monthly
   3. Biochemical tests : Monthly
   4. Autopsy : At the end of 90 days

# A CLINICAL STUDY TO EVALUATE THE THERAPEUTIC EFFECTS OF Linctus- 'H' IN LARYNGITIS

## INTRODUCTION

Once the therapeutic efficacy and safety of Linctus 'H' was conclusively established by experimental work in Rhesus monkeys suffering from Laryngitis, it was considered appropriate to extend the scope of this research work to human beings and hence a clinical trial was carried out in ten patients suffering from sore throat and laryngitis.

## MATERIAL AND METHODS

Ten patients attending Tasmia Clinic were selected for the study. The diagnosis of sore throat and laryngitis was made on the basis of clinical history, signs and symptoms.

Following symptoms were selected as parameters of the disease.

1. Pain/Soreness in Throat

2. Dry Cough
3. Fever
4. Pain during swallowing

Following Lab. Investigations were also carried out in all the ten patients.

3. Total Leukocyte count
4. Throat swab culture

The data are summarised in Table-1

## DISCUSSION

A double blind placebo controlled clinical study was carried out. Patients were randomly divided into two groups of five each. Group-I was put in placebo and Group-II was treated with Linctus-'H'.

After 24 hours of therapy, observation about relief in symptoms were recorded once after every 24 hours. Very obvious relief in symptoms was observed after 48 hours on initiation of therapy in patient treated with total extract. After 5 days out of 5 patients were completely free of symptoms. One patient showed improvement but was not fully well. In this case the medication was continued for further two days after which she was completely cured. Lab. Parameters of TLC and Throat swab culture were repeated after

## Table 1

| Pat. No. | Sex | Age | SYMPTOMS Pain in throat | Dry cough | Fever | Lab. Investigations TLC | Throat swab |
|---|---|---|---|---|---|---|---|
| 1. | M | 28 | Mild | + + + | Nil | 6840 | Positive |
| 2. | M | 42 | Moderate | + + + | M | 10200 | Negative |
| 3. | F | 34 | Moderate | + + + | L | 9110 | Positive |
| 4. | M | 46 | Severe | + + | H | 14000 | Positive |
| 5. | F | 22 | Mild | + + | M | 12800 | Positive |
| 6. | F | 45 | Severe | + + | H | 13400 | Positive |
| 7. | M | 51 | Severe | + + | H | 14700 | Positive |
| 8. | M | 28 | Mild | + + | M | 8600 | Negative |
| 9. | M | 38 | Moderate | + + + | L | 7200 | Positive |
| 10. | F | 19 | Moderate | + – | Nil | 7800 | Positive |

completion of therapy. TLC counts were found to be in normal range and throat swabs did not show any growth of pathogenic organisms.

Patients were also observed for untoward effects such as gastric upset, skin allergy, vomiting, cramps, headache or any other unpleasant side effects on appetite, general well beings and sleep. No side effects were observed.

In placebo group, three out of five patients showed worsening of symptoms and signs of disease, symptoms of two patients continued unchanged. None of the patient of the placebo group showed any relief in symptoms on fifth day of study. Patients of Group-II were reassessed one week after discontinuation of treatment. None showed any sign or symptoms of relapse of sore throat or laryngitis.

**Table 2. Response to treatment** (As assessed by Symptomatic Relief)

| | *Good* | *Fair* | *Poor* | *Worsening of Symptoms* |
|---|---|---|---|---|
| Group-I (Five cases) | – | – | 2 | 3 |
| Group-II (Five cases) | 4 | 1 | – | – |

## CONCLUSION

The present clinical study corroborates the findings of earlier study done on Rhesus monkeys and confirms the therapeutic efficacy of Linctus 'H' in sore throat and laryngitis in human beings.

# ANIMAL TOXICITY TESTS

## COURTESY C.D.R.I.

| *Test material* | *Animal species* | *Duration* | *Results* |
|---|---|---|---|
| Linctus-H | Rhesus monkeys | 90 days | Fully safe Non-toxic & *beneficial for the health |

* Proved by:

A. Increase in Haemoglobin

B. Decrease in Total Leukocyte Count

## *IN VIVO* EFFICACY TESTS IN MONKEYS

| *Test Material* | *Animal Species* | *Disease* | *Results* |
|---|---|---|---|
| Linctus-H | Rhesus monkeys | Laryngitis | More effective |

# Concluding Remarks

In the present study a phytomedicine Linctus 'H' was designed from three herbal ingredients namely Piper longum (fruit), Piper nigrum (fruit), Zingiber officinale (rhizome) and Honey. The preparation was standardized by advanced techniques such as spectrophotometry, chromatography and analytical tests. It was evaluated and tested for microbial contamination, toxicity studies and in vitro tests and animal models. On clinical trial it was found that Linctus 'H' exerts promising therapeutic effect in animals and humans and no side effect was observed. Clinical trials proved that Linctus 'H' is potent, safe and effective phytomedicine for curing laryngitis.

Thus it is concluded that if a phytomedicine is designed with a holistic approach by using such ingredients which are fruits or seasonal plant crops in nature, it will not cause deforestation. This is a need of the time as in India alone our forests are reduced from 34% to 14% since 1950. India is a great treasure house of herbs of great value to health and our Vedas (Indian health textbooks) have invaluable reference of such treasure as Neem, Haldi and Bitter Gourd, which have a worldwide acknowledgement. Moreover chemicals and chemical processing which will minimize environmental pollution as well as eliminate hazards to the health of the workers.